An Old-Fashioned Christmas

Never a Christmas morning,
Never the old year ends,
But someone thinks of someone,
Old days, old times, old friends.

Ideals Publishing Corporation
Nashville, Tennessee

ART & PHOTOGRAPHS

4, New England Christmas, Currier and Ives; **7**, Family Farm, Isaac Geib/Grant Heilman Photography; **9**, Christmas Pantry, H. Armstrong Roberts; **10**, Hot Chocolate, John Walters; **13**, Christmas Table, Jessie Walker; **14**, Candlemaking, A Teufen/H. Armstrong Roberts; **17**, Christmas Stollen, Gerald Koser; **19**, Christmas Silver, Grant Heilman Photography; **20-21**, Winter on the Skating Pond in Central Park, C. Parsons/Currier and Ives, Superstock; **23**, Bringing Home the Tree, The Bettmann Archive; **24**, Christmas Wreath in Williamsburg, Grant Heilman Photography; **27**, Christmas Belles, Superstock; **29**, The Christmas Tree, Ralph Luedtke; **31**, Looking for Santa, Superstock; **33**, Christmas Stocking, Gerald Koser; **36**, Old-Fashioned Sled Run; **39**, Teddy Bear, Gerald Koser; **41**, Teddy Bear, back view, Gerald Koser; **43**, Christmas inside Pennsylvania Dutch Farmhouse, Grant Heilman Photography; **45**, Burning Pine and Holly, The Bettmann Archive; **46-47**, Trotter on the Snow, Currier and Ives, Superstock; **48**, A Home in the Country, Currier and Ives, Superstock; **51**, Christmas Sleigh Bells, Gerald Koser; **52**, Village Church, Danville, Vermont, H. Armstrong Roberts; **55**, Winter Woods; **57**, Winter Morning, Currier and Ives, Superstock; **59**, Choral Singers, The Bettmann Archive; **60**, Through a Winter Window, Gerald Koser; **62**, Carolers; **65**, The Holly and the Ivy, Gerald Koser; **67**, Christmas Eve outside Country Church, lithograph, The Bettmann Archive; **68**, Moon and Cupola, Bristol, New Hampshire, Johnson's Photography; **70-71**, Skating Pond, Superstock; **73**, Toys at Christmas, H. Armstrong Roberts; **75**, Street Scenes at Christmas in Williamsburg, Grant Heilman Photography; **77**, Evergreens in Winter; **79**, Family Gathering, The Bettmann Archive; **80**, Country Christmas Dining Room, Jessie Walker; **83**, Farmhouse Door, Grant Heilman Photography; **84**, Coming Home for Christmas; **86**, Old-Fashioned Christmas Card, Superstock; **88**, Ornaments on the Tree, Gerald Koser; **90-91**, Winter Morning in the Country, Currier and Ives, Superstock;**92**, The Governor's Palace, Williamsburg, Grant Heilman Photography; **94**, Christmas Cookies, Gerald Koser; **96**, Christmas Kitchen, Jessie Walker; **99**, Tastes of Christmas, H. Armstrong Roberts; **100**, Christmas Candy, Gerald Koser; **103**, Christmas Sweets, H. Armstrong Roberts; **105**, Christmas Dinner, Grant Heilman Photography; **107**, The Hearth, A. Tuefen, H. Armstrong Roberts; **108-109**, Winter Scene,Currier and Ives; **111**, The Tree and Stockings, Gerald Koser; **113**, Hanging My Stocking, The Bettmann Archive; **114**, Gifts and Candles, H. Armstrong Roberts; **116**, Christmas Shopping, The Bettmann Archive; **119**, Ornaments, Gerald Koser; **121**, Old-Fashioned Ads at Christmas; **123** Homemade Wrappings, Gerald Koser; **125**, Wrapping Materials, Gerald Koser; **127**, Christmas Cards, Superstock; **128**, Happy Christmas to Mama and Papa/Old-Fashioned Santas. Jessie Walker; **130**, Children at Christmas; **132**, The Family Christmas Tree, woodcut, The Bettmann Archive; **134**, Winter Pastimes, Currier and Ives, Superstock; **136-137**, The Arrival for the Christmas Party, James R. Cooper, Superstock; **139**, Desk and Bible, Grant Heilman Photography; **141**, Winter Woods; **142**, Christmas Greetings; **144**, Decorating the Tree, The Bettmann Archive; **147**, Village Church in the Snow, Alexandria, New Hampshire, Johnson's Photography; **149**, Stained Glass, Laatsch-Hupp Photography; **150**, Church Organ, H. Armstrong Roberts; **153**, United Church, Milwaukee, Wisconsin, Barbara Laatsch-Hupp, Laatsch-Hupp Photography; **154**, Front Doors with Wreaths and Stained Glass, Tamworth, New Hampshire, Johnson's Photography; **156**, The Lighted Tree, H. Armstrong Roberts; **158**, Village on a Winter Night, H. Armstrong Roberts.

ACKNOWLEDGMENTS

Excerpt from ONCE UPON A CHRISTMAS by Pearl S. Buck. Copyright © 1972 by Creativity, Inc. Reprinted by permission of HarperCollins Publishers Inc. IN THE WEEK WHEN CHRISTMAS COMES from *Eleanor Farjeon's Poems for Children*. Originally appeared in *Come Christmas* by Eleanor Farjeon. Copyright 1927, 1955 by Eleanor Farjeon and reprinted by permission of HarperCollins Publishers. FOR CHRISTMAS from *Poems* by Rachel Field. Reprinted with permission of Macmillan Publishing Company (New York: Macmillan, 1957). A BOY AT CHRISTMAS by Edgar A. Guest. Used by permission of the author's estate. FOR OUR CHILDREN from *The Prayers of Peter Marshall*, compiled and edited by Catherine Marshall, copyright © 1949, 1950, 1951, 1954 by Catherine Marshall. Renewed 1982. Published by Chosen Books, Fleming H. Revell Company. Used by permission. THE MEANING OF CHRISTMAS from the writings of Bishop Fulton J. Sheen. Used by the permission of Propagation of the Faith. CHRISTMAS CAROL from *Collected Poems of Sara Teasdale* (New York: Macmillan, 1937). Our sincere thanks to the following whom we were unable to contact: Virginia Covel Boswell for A CHILD'S FACE, Vincent Godfrey Burns for SONNET TO CHRISTMAS, Anne Campbell for AN OLD-FASHIONED SLEIGH RIDE, Betty Cook for IT'S CHRISTMAS, Annette Patton Cornell for TWELFTH NIGHT, Marguerite Gode for CHRISTMAS MEMORIES, Herbert H. Hines for A CHRISTMAS PRAYER, Gertrude Bryson Holman for SIGNS OF CHRISTMAS, Frank H. Keith for LET US GO BACK, Adelaide Love for NO SWEETER THING, Truda McCoy for CHRISTMAS NIGHT, Catherine Parmenter for CHRISTMAS EVE, Alice Kennelly Roberts for CHRISTMAS DINNER, and Ann Silva for CHRISTMAS ON THE OLD FARM PLACE.

Text copy set in Palatino; Display type set in Tiffany
Color separations by Rayson Films, Waukesha, Wisconsin
Printed and bound by Ringier America, Milwaukee, Wisconsin

CONTENTS

THE
SCENTS OF CHRISTMAS

Gingerbread men in the pantry
And fruitcakes in the jar
Teased our noses constantly—
Christmas could not be far!

Christmas on the Old Farm

Only a few more days remain before Christmas, and the sounds, the tastes, the smells, and the joys that they bring to the farm. Outside, in the frosty cold farmyard, stands the old smokehouse, weathered a silver gray. Inside the smokehouse are the smells of Grandma's homemade soap, kept in the first room along with hoes, shovels, sickles, and kegs of nails. In the darkened room in the back are hams, sausages, and salted meats in crocks.

Inside the white frame walls of the farmhouse, hands large and small are busy cleaning and dusting and polishing everything in sight. Silver begins to gleam and sparkle in the gentle light of the fire. Syrup pitchers are full, and the pantry is stocked with apples, pies, cakes, and chocolate fudge loaded with nuts. And there are plenty of Grandma's homemade dill pickles—how we children love them!

In the parlor, the old pump organ is opened, decorated for the season with fresh-scented pine and holly boughs. The tree stands in the corner, trimmed with glitter and polished apples and oranges wrapped in tissue paper and tied with red ribbons. The tree will be lit—only on Christmas Eve, and only for a short while—by homemade candles. But we do not need the lights on the tree to tell us it is Christmas; its aroma, mingled with that of the bayberry candles, fills the room, and we know for certain that it is Christmastime on the old family farm.

Ann Silva

No Calendar Needed

For many years a calendar
Hung on our kitchen wall
And Mother checked the busy days
And seasons as they'd fall;
But no calendar was needed
To know the time of year—
By the fragrance of her kitchen
I knew the season near.

The aroma of hot chile
When wintry air blew cold;
The rhubarb custards cooling
When spring's magic would unfold;
Bubbling jellies in the kettle
When the summer heat was high;
And in frosty, tangy autumn
Whiffs of spicy pumpkin pie!

True, no calendar was needed
For an eager child to know
That Christmastime was coming!
Mother hurried to and fro
Making special sugar cookies
And our maple sugar candy;
While she whistled Christmas carols,
We knew everything was dandy.

Gingerbread men in the pantry
And fruitcakes in the jar
Teased our noses every minute—
Christmas could not be far!
We cracked nutmeats on the flatiron
And strung popcorn for the tree,
And every hour was heaven
In the kitchen, it seemed to me.

Mother in her big white apron,
With some flour on her cheek
Is the dearest recollection
Of my cherished Christmas week.
A calendar was useless,
There was no need for guessin'
For we always knew it was Christmas
By the fragrance of our kitchen.

Lolita Pinney

Hot Chocolate on Christmas Eve

After a round of caroling on a frosty Christmas Eve, a piping hot mug of hot chocolate was always a welcome treat. We'd step through the doorway, shake the snow from our boots, mittens, and hats, and follow the sweet aroma of chocolate into the parlor where Mother was waiting with cups full of warm chocolate to chase the chill of winter. I never let a Christmas pass without pulling out Mother's hot chocolate recipes.

Old-Fashioned Hot Chocolate

Blend two tablespoonfuls HERSHEY'S Cocoa, three tablespoonfuls granulated sugar, and a dash of salt in a one-and-a-half-quart saucepan. Gradually stir in a quarter-cup of hot water. Boil over medium heat for two minutes, stirring constantly. Add a cup and a half of milk and heat thoroughly, stirring occasionally. <u>Do not boil</u>. Remove from heat and beat with a rotary beater until foamy. Serve hot. Top with marshmallows or marshmallow whip. Yields about three six-ounce servings.

Mulled Hot Chocolate

Scald two quarts milk with one teaspoonful cinnamon, one half-teaspoonful nutmeg, and a quarter-teaspoonful cloves. Set aside. In a large kettle, bring four cups of water to a boil. Mix one half-cupful HERSHEY'S Cocoa with one cupful granulated sugar and one half-teaspoonful of salt; stir into boiling water. Boil five minutes. Combine mixtures, beating with a wire whisk; add two teaspoonfuls vanilla or one teaspoonful almond extract. Beat two minutes until frothy. Pour into mugs, sprinkle with shredded almonds, and serve instantly. Makes sixteen six-ounce servings.

Royal Hot Chocolate

Melt two squares HERSHEY'S Unsweetened Baking Chocolate in top of a double boiler over simmering water. Gradually add fourteen ounces of condensed milk and four cups boiling water, stirring constantly. Add one teaspoon vanilla extract. Ladle into mugs; top with a dollop of whipped cream and a dusting of cinnamon. Makes seven six-ounce servings.

Christmas Fragrance

It's Christmastime at our house,
Anyone could tell;
Even if you couldn't see
You'd know it by the smell.

There's fragrant air a-drifting;
It's loaded with good sniffs
Of gingerbread and popcorn
And baking cookie whiffs.

The kitchen's full of odors
Of pudding, steam, and cake—
And lots of other goodies
Mother likes to make.

There's aroma from the greens too
That mingles with the rest;
But if the truth be really told,
I like food fragrance best.

For I think the Christmas bouquet
Is a treat that's hard to beat
With its tantalizing promise
Of the things we're going to eat.

Solveig Paulson Russel

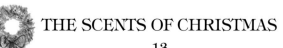

A Gift of Bayberry

It is said that if you burn a bayberry candle to the nub on Christmas Eve, you will have good luck for all the coming year. Bayberry candles are very fragile; but the scent that comes as you extinguish them will overcome any odor in the house, and they burn more evenly and with less smoke than tallow. They take time and patience to make, but are worth the effort, because their inimitable aroma will fill your home with the scent and flavor of an old-fashioned Christmas.

Wait until after the second frost, then collect as many bayberries as you can. You will need about two quarts for each candle, because only the thin skin of the berry yields wax. Discard the insides of the berries in the yard; the birds will find them in the cold, barren months of winter.

Once you have collected your berries, discard any that are black and boil the rest in a large kettle of water. Stir constantly or the aroma will boil away. After the water has come to a boil, set the pot aside to cool. The wax will rise to the top and you can skim it off with a spoon. Do not be discouraged by the appearance of the wax; it is very dark at this point but will change to a lovely green color later.

Remelt the skimmed wax in a copper kettle. (You must use copper if you want the wax to be green.) When the wax is melted, strain it through cheesecloth to remove impurities. Keep the wax in a covered container. Tie candle wicks to a candlerod and dip them into the hot bayberry wax as you would for tallow candles. After the second or third dip, let the candles cool slightly and straighten them with your fingers. The candles may crack slightly, but the wax from future dippings will yield a smooth taper. It takes about forty dips to make a good candle.
After they have dried, trim the bottoms with a sharp knife.
Bayberry candles are now ready to fill your home—or the home of a friend—with the wonderful aroma of Christmas.

Elizabeth Renes Heiss

Old-World Christmas Stollen

Stollen is bread dressed up for the holidays by a combination of fruit and nuts and sweeteners. Like the Christmas tree, Stollen came from Germany to America, where its sweet smell in the kitchen made families feel at home in the New World at holiday time.

To recreate the taste of Old-World Christmas Stollen, combine three cups of flour, two packages of dry yeast, a third of a cup of sugar, and one teaspoon of salt in a large mixing bowl; mix well. In a saucepan, heat one half-cup of milk, one half cup of water, and a third of a cup of butter until warm. Add to flour mixture. Add two eggs and blend until moistened. Beat with electric mixer three minutes at medium speed. By hand, gradually stir in a half cup of chopped candied cherries, a third of a cup of chopped citron, a quarter of a cup of raisins, and a quarter of a cup of pecans. Stir in two and half cups of flour to make a firm dough. Knead on a floured surface until smooth and elastic, five to ten minutes. Place in a greased bowl, turning to grease top. Cover and let rise in warm place until light and doubled, about one hour.

Punch dough; divide into two parts. On a lightly floured surface, roll or pat each half into an oval. Spread with softened butter. Fold in half lengthwise and curve into a crescent. Press folded edge firmly to seal. Place each half on a greased cookie sheet. Cover and let rise in a warm place until doubled in bulk, about thirty minutes.

Bake in a 350-degree preheated oven for twenty-five to thirty minutes until golden brown. Remove from cookie sheets.

Stir two tablespoons lemon or orange juice and one tablespoon vanilla into one cup confectioners' sugar. Add more juice, a teaspoon at a time until smooth enough to drizzle. Drizzle over top of warm stollen. Decorate with candied cherry halves and candied citron pieces.

Slice and serve. Cool remainder and wrap tightly.

It's Christmas

The table is spread for Christmas,
Bright in the light of the tree;
On the cloth a silver platter
Holds a turkey grand to see!
Hickory thighs and cinammon back
With drumsticks plump and tan
And cranberry tarts of crimson
Add a splash of color to the pan.

The children are opening presents
With paper all over the floor,
Each box brings a shriek of elation
As the contents they quickly explore.
Wagons of red and silver skates,
Making them eager to try;
Dolls that walk, with hair to curl,
And a plane that can really fly!

Someone has made a popcorn chain
And draped it in tinsel bright,
Carols are sung as the organ is pumped
In the flickering candlelight.
Eggnog thick with nutmeg top
Is served on a festive tray,
The tastes and the smells won't let us forget
That today is Christmas Day.

Betty Cooke

THE
SIGHTS OF CHRISTMAS

Now not a window small or big
But wears a wreath or holly sprig;
Nor any shop too poor to show
Its spray of pine or mistletoe.

THE SIGHTS OF CHRISTMAS

A World Full of Christmas

The stores are full of Christmas;
The streets are bright and gay;
On every hand
Throughout the land
Is Christmas on display.

But there's another Christmas
From all these things apart.
How sweet to know
That inner glow—
The Christmas of the heart!

Ruth Jenner

THE SIGHTS OF CHRISTMAS

For Christmas

Now not a window small or big
But wears a wreath or holly sprig;

Nor any shop too poor to show
Its spray of pine or mistletoe.

Now city airs are spicy sweet
With Christmas trees along each street,

Green spruce and fir whose boughs will hold
Their tinseled balls and fruits of gold.

Now postmen pass in threes and fours
Like bent, blue-coated Santa Claus.

Now people hurry to and fro
With little boys and girls in tow,

And not a child but keeps some trace
Of Christmas secrets in his face.

Rachel Field

An Old-Fashioned Sleigh Ride

Remember the thrill of the old-fashioned sleigh ride,
The straw in the sleigh and the bells ringing clear,
The road stretching white and the moon shining o'er us,
A hand in our own that was clinging and dear?

Perhaps there were ten of us there in the party,
Five boys and five girls that we liked best of all;
We planned for a square-dancing sociable evening
And spelling down too at the old Wickham Hall.

Remember the thrill of the old-fashioned sleigh ride,
The stretch of the country o'er which we must go;
The meadows so white and the houses so scattered,
The songs that we sang as we sped through the snow?

"Robin Adair" and "The Old Oaken Bucket,"
"Tenting Tonight" and "The Sweet By and By."
And all of us sang "When the Roll's Called up Yonder"
And smiled at the stars in the far-away sky.

Remember the thrill of the old-fashioned sleigh ride,
The lap robes of fur kept us cozy and warm;
The light in the window that beckoned us onward,
The hall when we reached it, its quaintness and charm?

Oh, talk as you like of our modern improvements,
Our autos are nice and their comfort is plain,
But, oh, to be young in the beautiful country
And ride in an old-fashioned sleigh once again!

Anne Campbell

The Christmas Tree

I have been looking on, this evening, at a merry company of children assembled round that pretty German toy, a Christmas tree. The tree was planted in the middle of a great round table, and towered high above their heads. It was brilliantly lighted by a multitude of little tapers; and everywhere sparkled and glittered with bright objects. There were rosy-cheeked dolls, hiding behind green leaves; there were real watches (with movable hands, at least, and an endless capacity of being wound up) dangling from innumerable twigs; there were French-polished tables, chairs, bedsteads, wardrobes, eight-day clocks, and various other articles of domestic furniture (wonderfully made in tin) perched among the boughs, as if in preparation for some fairy housekeeping; there were jolly broad-faced little men, much more agreeable in appearance than many real men—and no wonder, for their heads came off and showed them to be full of sugarplums; there were trinkets for the elder girls, far brighter than any grown-up gold and jewels; there were baskets and pin cushions in all devices; there were guns, swords, and banners; there were witches standing in enchanted rings of pasteboard, to tell fortunes; there were teetotums, humming-tops, needle cases, pen wipers, smelling bottles, conversation cards, bouquet holders, real fruit made artificially dazzling with gold leaf; imitation apples, pears, walnuts crammed with surprises; in short, as a pretty child before me delightedly whispered to another pretty child, her bosom friend, "There was everything, and more."

Charles Dickens

A Stocking Song on Christmas Eve

Welcome Christmas! heel and toe,
Here we wait three in a row.
Come good Santa Claus, we beg—
Fill us tightly, foot and leg.

Fill us quickly, 'ere you go,
Fill us till we overflow.
That's the way! and leave us more
Heaped in piles upon the floor.

Little feet that ran all day
Twitch in dreams of merry play;
Little feet that jumped at will
Lie all pink and warm and still.

See us, how we lightly swing;
Hear us, how we try to sing.
Welcome, Christmas, heel and toe,
Come and fill us 'ere you go.

Here we hang till someone nimbly
Jumps with treasure down the chimney.
Bless us! How he'll tickle us!
Funny old St. Nicholas!

Mary Mapes Dodge

The Art
of the
Christmas Stocking

Children have been hanging stockings above the fireplace on
Christmas Eve for generations; but while in the beginning the
stockings they hung were the simple wool socks they wore everyday,
it was not long before the Christmas stocking became a work of art itself.
Creative seamstresses and craftspeople used the rich colors and
fabrics of the holidays to transform the simple stocking hanging
by the chimney on Christmas Eve into a beautiful symbol of the joy
and celebration of the Christmas season.

This stocking, made from a rich burgundy velveteen lined with
deep rose taffetta and adorned with tapestry ribbon and jingle bells,
captures the spirit of an old-fashioned Christmas Eve.
Hang one by your own chimney, not just on Christmas Eve,
but throughout the holiday season.

To make this richly beautiful stocking a part of your own Christmas,
you will need a half-yard of velveteen and a half-yard of tafetta,
along with a remnant of batting large enough to cut a piece the size
of the stocking pattern. Also, choose in coordinating colors
a half-yard of tapestry ribbon, a half-yard of ruffled lace,
and two half-yards of satin ribbon in two colors. Six small bells will
help decorate the front of the stocking and give it a
lovely Christmas jingle.

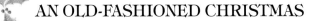

Reproduce the pattern provided onto a piece of tracing paper.
Each square on the graph is equivalent to one inch.
Pin the pattern piece to double thickness of the velveteen;
cut to create two matching pieces. Repeat with the tafetta,
again cutting two identical pieces.
Cut a single piece with the same pattern from the batting.
The pattern piece as drawn includes a half-inch seam allowance.

With right sides together, stitch the two velveteen stocking pieces together
around all but the top edge. Pin batting to wrong side of stocking front;
catch stitch to seams and across top at seam line. Turn down upper edge
of velveeen one half-inch toward wrong side. Baste. Turn
right side out and press lightly.

With wrong sides together, stitch the two lining pieces around all but top
edge. Trim seams. Turn down upper edge one half-inch toward wrong
side. Baste. Press. With wrong sides together, slip lining inside stocking;
slipstitch lining and stocking together across top.

Cut lengths of one color of the satin ribbon, lace, and tapestry ribbon to fit
around top of stocking. Sew satin ribbon on top of lace along unrufffled
edge; sew lace and ribbon strip to both long edges of tapestry ribbon.
Make a cuff out of tapestry strip and sew ends together. Pin to top of
stocking and hand stitch in place.

Trim stocking front with satin ribbon and jingle bells as shown. Make a
loop for hanging from two colors of satin ribbon and attach to back of
stocking top on inside. Hang the stocking by the chimney on Christmas
Eve and wait for the magic of the holiday to fill it to overflowing.

Mary E. Skarmeas

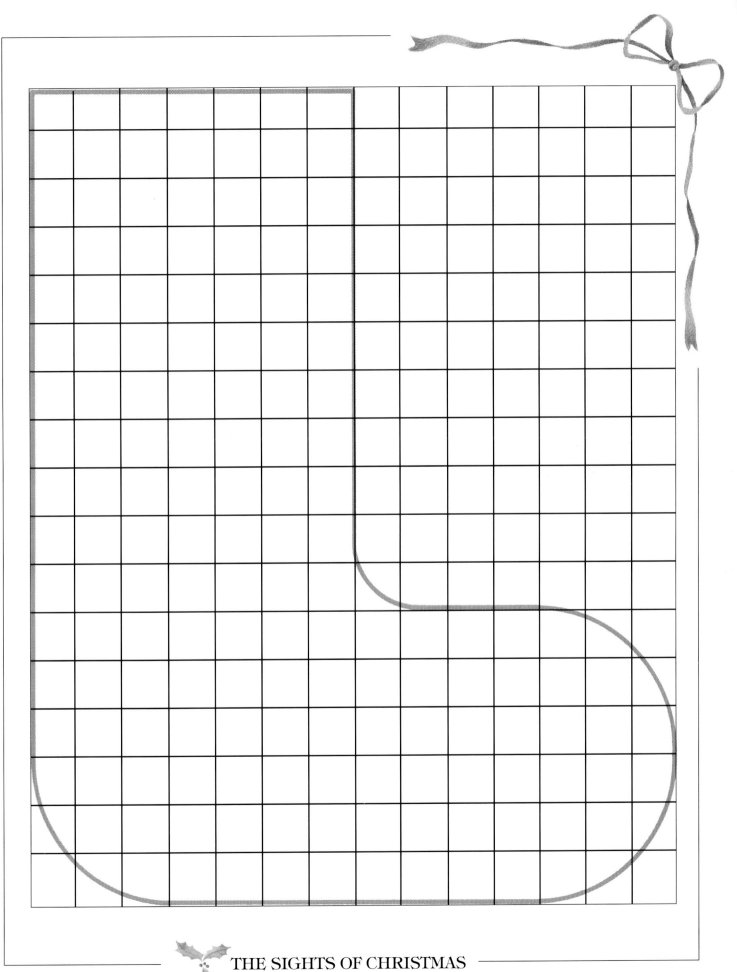

Christmas Sled

Oh, for the winters that used to be!
The winters that only a child may see!
Rich with the snowflakes' rush and swirl,
Keen as a diamond, pure as a pearl,
Brimming with healthful, rollicking fun,
Sweet with their rest when the play was done,
With kindly revels each day decreed,
And a Christmas sled for a royal steed.

Down from the crest with a shrill hurray!
Clear the track there, out of the way!
Scarcely touching the path beneath,
Scarce admitting of breath to breathe,
Dashing along, with leap and swerve,
Over the crossing, round the curve.
Talk of your flying machines! Instead,
Give me the swoop of that Christmas sled.

Author Unknown

A Teddy Bear
under the Tree
Christmas Morning

What child of any age or any country or any era does not love a teddy bear? The perfect sight for a child's eyes as he rushes to the tree on Christmas morning, the teddy bear becomes a playmate and friend unlike any other. This tiny teddy bear, made of lovely Australian boiled wool, is a classic example of this most beloved Christmas toy.

Our small, furry bear is made up of twenty-eight pieces cut from two colors of boiled wool, loden green for the body and light tan for the accents. The bear is assembled in pieces, with the head, body, arms, legs, and tail each put together and stuffed before joining together to make the finished bear.

You will need only an eighth of a yard of each color wool to make this bear, along with thread to match the wool, dark brown or black embroidery thread for the nose and mouth, and two purchased eyes. If you are making this bear for a young child, embroider the eyes; *do not use eyes that can be swallowed*. Trace the pattern pieces onto tracing paper; be sure to include the dotted lines—they indicate placement of legs, arms, eyes, nose, and eyelids. Also, note those pieces marked "2nd fabric" as this indicates that the piece be cut from the accent color.

Once the pieces are cut, begin to assemble the head. Refer to the photographs and drawings for placement and attach the pieces by pinning wrong sides together and hand sewing seams. Because the boiled wool does not ravel or fray, there is no seam allowance; simply stitch edge to edge. When head has been assembled, baste along neck edge and leave ends of thread long enough for tying; stuff head and pull together basted edge tightly; tie ends.

Repeat this process for the body, once again basting along neck edge and drawing together tightly. Assemble legs and arms and tail in a similar fashion; do not baste and tie openings. Sew ear pieces together but do not stuff.

When each body part has been sewn and stuffed, assemble bear. First sew together the head and body at neck where both pieces have been gathered. Next, attach arms and legs, using dotted lines on pattern pieces as a guide to placement. Sew on tail, ears, and eyebrows. Glue eyes in place, or embroider, and embroider nose and mouth.

Susan Harrison

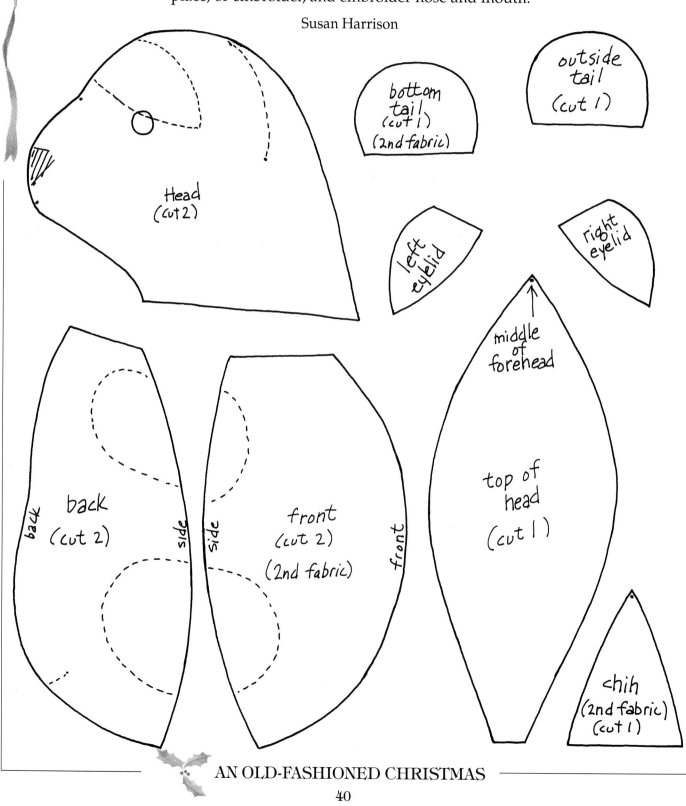

outside
leg
(cut 2)

pad
of
foot
(cut 2)
(2nd fabric)

inside
leg
(cut 2)

outside
arm
(cut 2)

front of
ear
(cut 2)
(2nd fabric)

back
of
ear
(cut 2)

paw
(cut 2)
(2nd fabric)

inside
arm
(cut 2)

We Light a Candle

We light a candle on Christmas Eve,
And in its glow I do believe
We catch a glimpse of the Wondrous Light
Which came to earth that holy night

When Christ was born in Bethlehem
And wise men came to worship Him,
And angels sang with joy on high
From out a distant, star-lit sky.

We light a candle on Christmas Eve;
It flickers in the air we breathe.
Fragments of the light Divine
We pause to ponder the heavenly shine.

The golden light, so freely given,
Is meant to guide our way to heaven;
And thus we honor Him this way
By burning candles on Christmas Day.

Minnie Klemme

A Catch
by the Hearth

Sing we all merrily
Christmas is here,
The day that we love the best
Of days in the year.

Bring forth the holly,
The box and the bay,
Deck out our cottage
For glad Christmas-day.

Sing we all merrily,
Draw around the fire,
Sister and brother,
Grandson and sire.

Sing we all merrily
Christmas is here,
The day that we love the best
Of days in the year.

Author Unknown

THE
SOUNDS OF CHRISTMAS

Sounds of Christmas fill the air.
Sleigh bells jingle everywhere,
Moonlight glistening on falling snow,
Cozy warm fireplaces all aglow.

THE SOUNDS OF CHRISTMAS

It's Christmas

Sounds of Christmas fill the air.
Sleigh bells jingle everywhere,
Moonlight glistening on falling snow,
Cozy warm fireplaces all aglow.

Bright-ribboned packages under the tree;
Santa is coming tonight, you see.
Children's laughter, sweet to hear;
Faces radiant with Christmas cheer.

Turkey, pudding, and gay-bedecked trees;
Everyone trying so hard to please.
Carolers singing o'er the still of the night,
Proclaiming to all the world is right.

Christ Child above smiles over all;
Hearts tuned to Heaven, awaiting his call.

Ruby D. Kish

The Bells

Hear the sledges with the bells,
Silver bells!
What a world of merriment their melody foretells!
How they tinkle, tinkle, tinkle,
In the icy air of night!
While the stars that oversprinkle
All the heaven seem to twinkle
With a crystalline delight;
Keeping time, time, time,
In a sort of Runic rhyme,
To the tintinabulation that so musically wells
From the bells, bells, bells, bells,
Bells, bells, bells—
From the jingling and the tinkling of the bells.

Edgar Allan Poe

THE SLEIGH RACE.

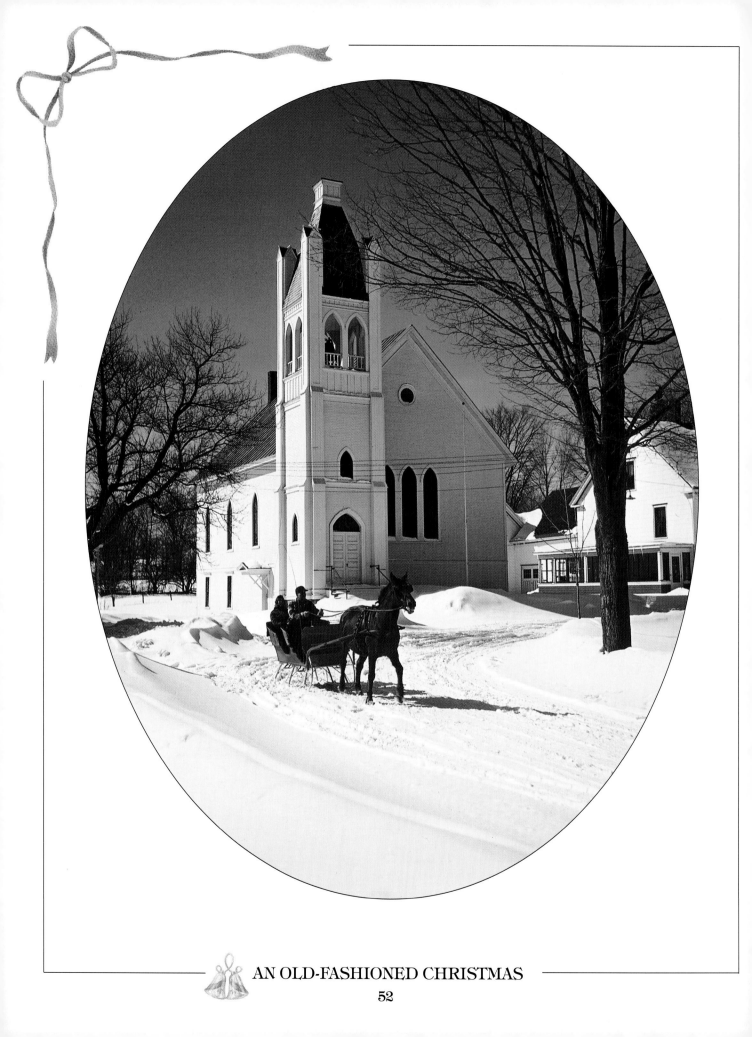

Christmas Bells

I heard the bells on Christmas Day
Their old, familiar carols play,
And wild and sweet
The words repeat
Of peace on earth, good-will to men!

And thought how, as the day had come,
The belfries of all Christendom
Had rolled along
The unbroken song
Of peace on earth, good-will to men!

Till, ringing, singing on its way,
The world revolved from night to day,
A voice, a chime,
A chant sublime
Of peace on earth, good-will to men!

Then pealed the bells more loud and deep:
"God is not dead; nor doth he sleep!
The Wrong shall fail,
The Right prevail,
With peace on earth, good-will to men!

Henry Wadsworth Longfellow

Christmas Is Quiet

Christmas is quiet,
A hush in the air.

Christmas is peace,
Hearts full of prayer.

Christmas is joyful,
A child's smiling face.

Christmas is love
A dear one's embrace.

Christmas is kindness,
To give generously.

Christmas is always
If we wish it to be.

Violet Bigelow Rourke

The Sweetest Sounds of Christmas

The sweetest sounds
Of Christmas
Aren't the carols,
Old and dear,
Not the jingling
Of the sleighbells
Or the church bells
Pealing clear.

The sweetest sounds
Of Christmas
Are the melodies
That start
As thoughts of peace
And kindness
Within
A loving heart.

Constance Hiser

Wassail Song

Traditional.

Old English

mf Moderato

1. Here we come a was-sailing A-mong the leaves so green;
2. We are not daily beg-gars That beg from door to door; But
3. God bless the master of this house, Like-wise the mistress, too, And

Here we come a wan-d'ring, So fair to be seen.

we are neighbors' children, Whom you have seen be-fore. Love and joy come to

all the little children, That round the table go.

f Refrain

you, And to you your wassail too; And God bless you and send you a

hap-py New Year, And God send you a happy New Year.

Christmas Night

Snowflakes dancing,
Flying, falling,
All the world is white;
I hear the happy
Children calling,
"It is Christmas night!"

I hear the happy
Children singing
Carols sweet and clear:
I hear the church bells
Ringing, ringing
Christmas night is here.

Truda McCoy

Christmas Carols

Wake me that I, The twelvemonth long,
May bear the song
About me in the world's great throng;

That treasured joys of Christmastide
May with mine hour of gloom abide;

The Christmas carol ring
Deep in my heart when I would sing,

Each of the twelve good days,
In earnest yield of duteous love and praise
Ensuring happy months
And hallowing common ways.

John Keble

The Holly and the Ivy

Traditional

French
Arranged by Sir John Stainer

1. The hol-ly and the i — vy, Now both are full well grown, Of
2. The hol-ly bears a blos-som, As white as li-ly flow'r: And
3. The hol-ly bears a ber-ry, As red as any blood; And
4. The hol-ly bears a prickle, As sharp as any thorn; And

all the trees that are in the wood, The holly bears the crown.—
Ma-ry bore sweet Je-sus Christ, To be our sweet Sav-iour.—
Ma-ry bore sweet Je-sus Christ, To do poor sinners good.—
Ma-ry bore sweet Je-sus Christ, On Christmas Day in the morn.—

Refrain

O the ris-ing

of the sun, The run-ning of the deer, The playing of the merry organ, Sweet

sing-ing in the quire, Sweet sing-ing in the quire.

The Messiah

Comfort ye, comfort ye, my people, saith your God; speak ye comfortably to Jerusalem; and cry unto her, that her warfare is accomplished, that her iniquity is pardoned. The voice of him that crieth in the wilderness;— prepare ye the way of the Lord; make straight in the desert a highway for our God. Every valley shall be exalted, and every valley and hill made low, the crooked straight and the rough places plain. And the glory of the Lord shall be revealed, and all flesh shall see it together, for the mouth of the Lord hath spoken it.

Thus saith the Lord of Hosts:—Yet once a little while and I will shake the heavens and the earth, the sea and the dry land; and I will shake all nations; and the desire of all nations shall come. The Lord, whom you seek, shall suddenly come to His temple, even the messenger of the covenant, whom you delight in; behold, He shall come, saith the Lord of Hosts. But who may abide the day of His coming? and who shall stand when he appeareth? For He is like a refiner's fire. And he shall purify the sons of Levi, that they might offer unto the Lord an offering in righteousness.

Behold, a Virgin shall conceive and bear a Son, and shall call him Emmanuel, God with us. O thou that tellest good tidings to Zion, get thee up into the high mountain: O thou that tellest good tidings to Jerusalem, lift up thy voice with strength, lift it up, be not afraid; say unto the cities of Judah, Behold your God! Arise, shine, for thy light is come, and the glory of the Lord is risen upon thee.

For behold, darkness shall cover the earth, and gross darkness the people; but the Lord shall arise upon thee, and His glory shall be seen upon thee, and the Gentiles shall come to thy light, and kings to the brightness of thy rising. The people that walked in darkness have seen a great light; and they that dwell in the land of the shadow of death, upon them hath the light shined.

For unto us a Child is born, unto us a son is given, and the government shall be upon His shoulder, and His name shall be called Wonderful, Counsellor, The Mighty God, the Everlasting Father, The Prince of Peace. There were shepherds abiding in the field, keeping watch over their flocks by night. And lo! the Angel of the Lord came upon them, and the glory of the Lord shone round about them, and they were sore afraid. And the angel said unto them, fear not; for behold I bring you good tidings of great joy, which shall be to all people; for unto you is born this day in the city of David, a saviour, which is Christ the Lord.

And suddenly there was with the Angel a multitude of the heavenly host, praising God and saying: Glory to God in the highest, and peace on earth, goodwill towards men. Rejoice greatly, O daughter of Zion! Shout! O daughter of Jerusalem! behold, thy King cometh unto thee! He is the righteous Savior, and He shall speak peace unto the heathen.

Then shall the eyes of the blind be opened, and the ears of the deaf unstopped; then shall the lame man leap as an hart, and the tongue of the dumb shall sing.

He shall feed His flock like a shepherd; and He shall gather the lambs with His arms, and carry them in His bosom, and gently lead those that are with young. Come unto Him, all ye that labor and are heavy laden, and he will give you rest. Take His yoke upon you and learn of him, for He is meek and lowly of heart, and ye shall find rest unto your souls. His yoke is easy and His burthen is light.

Silent Night

Silent night! Holy night!
All is calm, all is bright,
'Round yon Virgin Mother and Child,
Holy Infant, so tender and mild,
Sleep in heavenly peace,
Sleep in heavenly peace.

Silent night! Holy night!
Son of God, love's pure light,
Radiant beams from thy heavenly face,
With the dawn of redeeming grace,
Jesus Lord at Thy birth.
Jesus Lord at Thy birth.

Silent night! Holy night!
Shepherds quake at the sight,
Glories stream from heaven afar,
Heavenly hosts sing "Alleluia;"
Christ the Saviour is born!
Christ the Saviour is born!

Joseph Mohr

THE
FEEL OF CHRISTMAS

Let us return to the Christmas
That remains with the children of time—
That Christmas of wonderful wishes,
Of stardust, and snowdrift, and chime!

THE FEEL OF CHRISTMAS

To an American Family at Christmas

Ah, Christmas! It goes back far, far into my memory; into the earliest years of my childhood. Christmas was the time when we were really American—my parents, my little sister, and I. There were many other festivals which we celebrated with our Chinese friends during the Chinese moon-year. There was even an English festival, the Queen's Birthday—Queen Victoria, of course—which we celebrated with the handful of English who lived in the British Concession, a strip of walled land along the Yangtze River.

Curiously enough, Christmas each year of my childhood began with a Christmas Eve party for all non-Chinese children, this party being given by a kindly English lady in the British Concession. I enjoyed the part because it was elaborately generous as to food and gifts, but my enjoyment was hampered by two facts: one, that we had to go in fancy costumes, which tortured my naturally shy self; and second, all my real friends were Chinese and I resented their exclusion. Mrs. Tamplin's parties were the beginning of each year's Christmas, nevertheless, and so continued until her Commissioner husband was retired or sent elsewhere—I do not know. But I do remember the magnificent house, the soft carpets and rich furniture, and the great, glittering tree.

Our own tree was small and much less loaded with gifts. But the gifts included those for our Chinese household and the things we children had made for our parents, at which they always expressed the proper appreciative surprise. And of course, theirs for us, brought presumably by Santa Claus from faraway America, via Montgomery Ward, from whom my parents ordered once a year such necessities as we could not buy in our Chinese city. When we ceased to believe in Santa Claus I do not know, but my inventive mother made the transition easy—so easy, in fact, that my first narrative poem was written on the subject. The poem was lost long ago, and I remember now merely my agony at my mother's requiring me to read it aloud to a group of her friends. Perhaps I even tore it up afterwards—I was capable of that, I fear.

Christmas dinner was, of course, an event. Turkey was unknown, but we had roast goose, with trimmings, preceded by the once-a-year-only oyster soup, a favorite dish of mine to this day, but rare in those days because oysters were imported in tin cans from foreign country—Australia?

England? perhaps even America! But wherever, that Christmas oyster
soup surpasses, in my memory, all subsequent ones.

We hung up our stockings and found them always delightfully
overflowing. These could be emptied and enjoyed before breakfast, but
the tree only after breakfast, and after my father, in his grave beautiful
voice, had read the Christ story. The tree came after that, usually a pretty
holly tree which an enterprising villager cut for us each year from the
nearby mountains, bringing also two great loads of lovely, richly berried
holly, one at each end of his carrying pole. Chinese holly
is the most beautiful in the world.

From such memories of my Chinese childhood, it is no wonder that when
I had an American home of my own, complete with husband and
children, every Christmas was as joyous as we could make it.

Pearl S. Buck

Christmas Eve

Pine-crowned hills against the sky,
Kneeling low to pray;
Friendly, lamp-lit villages
Along the snowbound way;
Myriads of silver stars
Gleaming softly bright . . .
Little King of Bethlehem
I see Thy star tonight!

Fragrant wreaths and candle-glow
In a city street,
Songs of Christmas carolers
High and clear and sweet—
Echoes of the angel host,
With wings of shining white . . .
Little King of Israel,
I hear Thy song tonight!

Words of ancient prophecy
Are mine to take or leave:
Visions of a golden age
This happy Christmas Eve.
Peace on earth, good-will to men—
Oh, dim and holy light! . . .
Little King of all the world,
I share thy dream tonight!

Catherine Parmenter

Carol

Villagers all, this frosty tide,
Let your doors swing open wide,
Though the wind may follow, and snow beside,
Yet draw us in by your fire to bide;
Joy shall be yours in the morning!

Here we stand in the cold and sleet,
Blowing fingers, stamping feet,
Come from faraway you to greet—
You by the fire and we in the street—
Bidding you joy in the morning!

For ere one half the night was gone,
Sudden a star has led us on,
Raining bliss and benison—
Bliss tomorrow and more anon,
Joy for every morning!

Goodman Joseph toiled through the snow—
Saw the star o'er a stable low;
Mary she might not further go—
Welcome thatch, and litter below!
Joy was hers in the morning!

And then they heard the angels tell
"Who was first to cry Nowell?
Animals all, as it befell,
In the stable where they did dwell!
Joy shall be theirs in the morning!"

Kenneth Grahame

THE FEEL OF CHRISTMAS

77

Mother's Christmas

The very name of December as it comes in sight on our calendars, or gazes at us from the newly turned pages of our almanacs, gives us a thrill of pleasure with its warm suggestion of Christmas greetings and festivities. Each Christmas brings its special delights, more sober and chastened as we learn to find our own joy in the happiness of others, instead of expecting others to provide it for us.

Christmas is indeed the children's feast; hallowed by the remembrance of the holy child born, as on this day, at Bethlehem. To every mother the thought of the virgin mother rejoicing over her firstborn, with no foreboding as yet of the sword which was to pierce her own soul, must come with a peculiar nearness that calls forth an answering glow of sympathy and tenderness.

The sword comes to each in turn. Even if the bitter trials of loss and bereavement are spared, the children go, the years steal them away. Let them be made happy while they stay. The tenderest love and the fullest indulgence can do them no harm if generosity and unselfishness are the lessons of their daily life, taught by precept and by example.

Gifts are the great consideration at Christmas. Thought of and dreamed of for weeks before by the children. Pondered over and worried over for more than the same length of time, by the busy mother of small means. Each of her darlings must have something, and how to bring the parents within the limit of the narrow income, which it is so hard to stretch to cover daily wants, is a puzzle that would bewilder the wisest head.

When there is not much money to spare do not fritter it away on a number of little things, but spend each one's share in some substantial gift that can be kept as a remembrance. It need not be intrinsically valuable, but let it be something that the child can keep with reasonable care, as a memento of the happy Christmas at home. A certain China box with figures of a girl and boy feeding chickens on the cover, that once delighted the heart of a little girl at five, is still, after nearly forty years, one of her chief treasures. The sight of the quaint coloring brings remembrances that are almost overpowering in their strength and sweetness. It is a fragment of the past, and precious as the last glimpse of the long vanished fairyland of sheltered childhood.

Mothers are making now the memories that are to be the inheritance of their children during all their lives. Let there be a few words of tenderness and blessing to recall when they look back with full hearts on those happy Christmas mornings. Let the sound of one of the grand old hymns that have expressed the Christmas joy of so many generations mingle with them. Its music will then always bring the echo of the voice that made the very center and core of home.

The touch of solemnity will not dampen the children's mirth, only soften and sweeten it, making the day, in the truest sense of the dear words of greeting—A merry Christmas.

Elisabeth Robinson Scovil
Ladies' Home Journal 1890

Christmas Memories

We gathered all our packages
And climbed aboard the train
And off to Grandmama's we went
At Christmastime again.
Past fields and woodlands bright in snow
From station on to station,
We chugged our merry way along
To reach the destination—
And there was Grandpa!

A furry cap perched on his head,
His whiskers long and white,
His face wreathed in a dimpled smile
He was a welcome sight.
Up busy little streets we trudged
Past home and churches lighted
Until we came to one big house
And oh, were we delighted—
There was Grandmama!

The smell of supper filled the air,
The room was warm and cozy
With Grandmama bustling around
Her two cheeks red and rosy.
Inside the parlor stood the tree
To rouse anticipation,
And sacks of bundles heralding
Tomorrow's celebration—
It was Christmas Eve!

With emptied stockings by the grate
And floors adrift in litter
Of ribbon bows and tinsel balls
That now had shed their glitter.
The old house was a friendly spot,
A place for family meeting,
With friends and neighbors dropping in
To share the yuletide greeting—
It was Christmas Day!

Marguerite Gode

Home for Christmas

The folks are coming home for Christmas
All the windows are aglow;
We have a tree and wreaths and candles
And we have some snow!

There are gifts upon the mantel
And there are gifts beneath the tree;
The whole house is breathing Christmas
And so by now are we.

Do I hear sleigh bells in the distance?
We're waiting from cellar to dome.
Hurrah, hurrah, a merry Christmas—
The folks are finally home!

Minnie Klemme

Home at Christmastime

Christmas is the best time of year to be home. The holidays, though greeted by Mother Nature with an embrace of chill winds and vistas turning white with snow, are full of special moments meant for sharing. A fire blazes hot in the stone fireplace and boughs of fresh-cut pine line the mantel, filling the entire house with the scent of the forest. A bit of mistletoe, tied with a bright red ribbon, dangles provocatively over the doorway. There are baskets filled with rich treats for friends and neighbors, and pretty dishes filled with sweets for the family.

Carols echo from every street corner, mulled cider stays warm by the fire, and chestnuts roast on the hearth. Snowflakes drift out of the silent night sky, the windows are artfully decorated by the lacy fingers of Jack Frost, and crystal icicles sparkle along the eaves of the house. A huge pine tree dominates the room, its limbs heavy with strings of popcorn and cranberries, glass ornaments, and shiny tinsel. At the very top of the tree the little angel's porcelain eyes watch the activity of the season unfold below her, as they have done since my great-grandfather was a child. Presents, wrapped in an array of reds, blues, greens, and golds, are piled beneath the tree to await tomorrow morning when the family will gather to rip and tear through the ribbon and tape to discover what St. Nicholas left them this year.

Woven from the fabric of these traditions is a rich tapestry of memories that makes Christmas and home inseparable for me.

Kathy Jones

A MERRY CHRISTMAS

This little card
has come to say:
"Merry be your
Christmas Day."

Let Us Go Back

Let us go back to the beauties
That are pocketed deep in our past—
The joys we relinquished with childhood
But which hauntingly linger and last!
Let us return to the Christmas
That remains with the children of time—
That Christmas of wonderful wishes,
Of stardust and snowdrift and chime!

Let us go back to the vision
Of evergreen peace in our rooms,
Gay ribbons on gifts of the giving,
And the dream that consistently blooms!
Let us in piety wander
Where the veil of the centuries parts
To look at a Crib and an Infant,
And Christmas will live in our hearts!

Frank H. Keith

In the Week When Christmas Comes

This is the week when Christmas comes.

Let every pudding burst with plums,
And every tree bear dolls and drums,
In the week when Christmas comes.

Let every hall have boughs of green
With berries glowing in between,
In the week when Christmas comes.

Let every doorstep have a song
Sounding the dark street along,
In the week when Christmas comes.

Let every steeple ring a bell
With a joyful tale to tell,
In the week when Christmas comes.

Let every night put forth a star
To show us where the heavens are,
In the week when Christmas comes.

Let every stable have a lamb
Sleeping warm beside its dam,
In the week when Christmas comes.

This is the week when Christmas comes.

Eleanor Farjeon

THE
TASTE OF CHRISTMAS

Yes, hearts go home at Christmas
To take again their place,
To see at Christmas dinner
Each dear remembered face . . .

A Christmas Carol

God bless the master of this house,
The mistress also,
And all the little children,
That round the table go.

And all your kin and folk,
That dwell both far and near;
I wish you a merry Christmas,
And a happy new year.

Old English Carol

Old-Fashioned Sugar Cookies

Decorated sugar cookies have always been a part of the American Christmas celebration. As with most things, the old way is the best; sugar cookies made with a simple, old-fashioned recipe can't be beat. Made in the traditional shapes of Christmas—trees, angels, wreaths, or Santas—sugar cookies can be decorated treat, a gift for a friend, or colorful ornaments for your tree.

Sift three cups unbleached, all-purpose flour with one-half teaspoon baking powder and one-half teaspoon salt. Set aside. Cream one cup butter with one cup sugar until light and fluffy. Add one teaspoon vanilla extract and two eggs, one at a time, beating after each addition. Stir in dry ingredients. Wrap tightly and refrigerate three to four hours.

Preheat the oven to 350 degrees. On a lightly floured board, roll one fourth of the dough to about one-quarter-inch thickness. Cut out with cookie cutters in Christmas shapes dipped in flour. Arrange cookies on ungreased cookie sheet one inch apart. Bake eight to ten minutes or just until edges are golden. Remove to wire rack to cool. Decorate with Icing and colored sugar and nonpareils. Makes four dozen.

Icing

Combine one pound confectioners' sugar, one tablespoon softened butter, and one-half teaspoon almond extract. Stir in one-third cup of milk, a small amount at a time until mixture is of spreading consistency. To tint icing, divide into small bowls and add small amounts of food coloring until desired colors are achieved.

Note: To make cookie tree decorations, press both ends of a clean six-inch length of string into top of cookie before baking.

Dory Morley

Signs of Christmas

It's beginning to look like Christmas!
The candle in the window bright,
Like the star in the heavens above,
Still glows to guide good folks at night.

A little tree stands proudly there
Draped in silvery glittering snow,
With colored lights and tinsel too
And above them all, a star to glow.

There's laughter and love and beautiful speech
And the echo of lively bouncing feet,
As warmly clad children romp and play
As they troop merrily down the street.

In the country, barns are filled
And pantry shelves are laden down;
The tables are heaped with fruit and nuts
And in the oven, mincemeat brown.

For in our homes it is Christmastime
With merry voices of the children;
We all join hands and sing a hymn
For peace and good will toward all men!

Gertrude Bryson Holman

Christmas Sweets
Apricot Snowballs

The tastes of an old-fashioned Christmas aren't limited to the goose and its fixings at Christmas dinner; the season has always been full of special sweet treats, from fruitcake to marzipan to gingerbread men. Apricot snowballs, delicious balls of fruit and nuts and sugar, are treats too rich and wonderful for any season but Christmas, and an old-fashioned tradition worth reviving.

Begin your apricot snowballs using a rolling pin to crush two cups of cereal flakes between two sheet of wax paper. Stir the crushed flakes with a third of a cup of pitted dates, two thirds a cup of dried apricots, and a half cup of chopped pecans in a large bowl until combined. In a small pan, melt a quarter cup of honey and three tablespoons of butter. Stir in one teaspoon of vanilla extract. Pour the liquid mixture over the cereal flake mixture and mix thoroughly. Chill for thirty minutes. Form balls from tablespoons of mixture; roll each ball in sugar and garnish with a strip of apricot or a cherry half. Serve immediately or cover and chill until needed.

Candy Shop
at Christmastime

The candy shop at Christmastime
Is a very favorite place
Of all the children everywhere
Come to choose from the candy case.

The silver bell atop the door
Tinkles a merry Christmas song,
Reminding the friendly storekeeper
Of the Christmas season all day long.

Red and white striped candy canes
In wide jars sparkling clean,
Nutty chunks of chocolate fudge—
The thickest I have ever seen.

Snowy white mounds of divinity,
Golden chips of buttered rum;
The spicy smell of cinnamon balls
And every flavor of fruity gum.

How puzzled are these shining eyes
Of children, each clutching a dime,
Trying to make the wisest choice
In the candy shop at Christmastime.

Ruth Underhill

Visions of Sugarplums

The children were nestled all snug in their beds
While visions of sugarplums danced in their heads.

A Visit from St. Nicholas
Clement Moore

It is no wonder that children once dreamed of sugarplums at Christmastime. These wonderfully sweet little balls of nuts and fruit were a luxury out of the question in any other season. But at Christmas parents indulged their children, and their dreams of rich, sweet sugarplums more often than not came true.

To make sugarplums worth dreaming about, chop one pound figs, one pound dates, one pound raisins, one pound currants; set aside. Chop one pound blanched almonds, one-half pound walnuts, one-half pound pecans, and one pound unsalted, shelled pistachio nuts; set aside. Combine one-half pound shredded coconut, one-half pound crystallized ginger, the grated rind and juice of one orange and one lemon, two tablespoons sherry, and one ounce orange or peach brandy until thoroughly mixed. Combine the fruit and nuts; add the juice, sherry, and brandy mixture. Mix thoroughly. Form into small balls and roll in granulated sugar. Store in covered tin lined with wax paper for one week to let flavors blend.

Christmas Dinner

The heart remembers Christmas
And days of long ago,
When festive preparations
Made all the house aglow;
The kitchen fairly bubbled
With turkey, puddings, pies,
And all those extra goodies
Which came as a surprise.

Each person had his duties,
And old and young could share,
The little ones, and Grandma
And even "Sport" was there;
The fruitcake and the mincemeat,
The chestnut dressing too;
The pumpkins and red apples
Filled childhood's world anew.

Yes, hearts go home at Christmas
To take again their place,
To see at Christmas dinner
Each dear remembered face;
And though the scene we cherish
Is no longer there,
The word, the joys, the laughter
Are with us through the years.

Alice Kennelly Roberts

Christmas Goose
at the Cratchits

You might have thought a goose the rarest of all birds; a feathered phenomenon, to which the black swan was a matter of course; and in truth, it was something like it in that house. Mrs. Cratchit made the gravy (ready before hand in a little saucepan) hissing hot; Master Peter mashed the potatoes with incredible vigor; Miss Belinda sweetened up the applesauce; Martha dusted the hot plates; Bob took Tiny Tim beside him in a tiny corner, at the table; the two young Cratchits set chairs for everybody, not forgetting themselves, and mounting guard upon the posts, crammed spoons into their mouths, lest they should shriek for goose before their turn came to be helped. At last the dishes were set on, and grace was said. It was succeeded by a breathless pause as Mr. Cratchit, looking slowly all along the carving knife, prepared to plunge it in the breast; but when he did, and the long-expected gush of stuffing issued forth, one murmur of delight arose all around the board, and even Tiny Tim, excited by the two young Cratchits, beat on the table with the handle of his knife and feebly cried, hurrah!

There was never such a goose. Bob said he didn't believe there was ever such a goose cooked. Its tenderness and flavor, size and cheapness, were themes of universal admiration. Eked out by the applesauce and mashed potatoes, it was sufficient dinner for the whole family; indeed, as Mrs. Cratchit said with great delight (surveying one small atom of a bone on the dish), they hadn't eaten it all at last! Yet everyone had had enough, and the youngest Cratchits in particular were steeped in sage and onion to the eyebrows!

At last the dinner was all done, the cloth was cleared, the hearth swept, and the fire made up. . . . Then all the Cratchit family drew around the hearth . . . Then Bob proposed:

"A merry Christmas, to us all, my dears. God bless us!" Which all the family re-echoed.

"God bless us everyone!" said Tiny Tim, the last of all.

Charles Dickens

THE
SECRETS OF CHRISTMAS

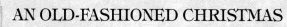

Life holds no sweeter thing than this—to tell
A little child, while Christmas candles glow,
The story of a Babe whose humble birth
Became the loveliest of truths we know.

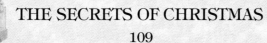

A Christmas Prayer

We open here our treasures
And our gifts;
And some of it is gold,
And some is frankincense,
And some is myrrh;
For some has come from plenty,
Some from joy,
And some from deepest
Sorrow of the soul.

But Thou, O God, dost know
The gift is love,
Our pledge of peace,
Our promise of good will.
Accept the gift
And all the life we bring.

Herbert H. Hines

 THE SECRETS OF CHRISTMAS

The Joy of Giving

Somehow, not only for Christmas
But all the long year through,
The joy that you give to others
Is the joy that comes back to you;

And the more you spend in blessing
The poor and lonely and sad,
The more of your heart's possessing
Returns to make you glad.

John Greenleaf Whittier

A Christmas Carol

The Kings they came from out the South,
All dressed in Ermine fine;
They bore Him gold and chrysoprase,
And gifts of precious wine.

The Kings they knocked upon the door;
The Shepherds entered in;
The Wise Men followed after them,
To hear the song begin.

The Wise Men came from out the East,
And they were wrapped in white:
The star that led them all the way
Did glorify the night.

The Shepherds came from out the North,
Their coats were brown and old;
They brought Him little new-born lambs—
They had not any gold.

The Angels came from heaven high,
And they were clad with wings;
And lo! they brought a joyful song
The host of heaven sings.

The Angels sang all through the night,
Until the rising sun,
But little Jesus fell asleep
Before the song was done.

Sara Teasdale

Shopping Before Christmas

The streets are bright in Christmas-town,
Beyond the frosted pane,
Where merchants sell their trinkets down
Each avenue and lane.

The bells sound through the falling snow
Like voices drifting far,
From where the lights of heaven glow
And God's own candles are.

Walk softly through the crowded mart,
Nor linger for a word;
Look up, and hear within your heart
The song the Shepherds heard.

Ruth Gibbs Zwall

The Gift of the Magi

One dollar and eighty-seven cents. That was all. And sixty cents of it was in pennies. Three times Della counted it. One dollar and eighty-seven cents. And the next day would be Christmas. There was clearly nothing to do but flop down on the shabby little couch and howl. So Della did it.

Della finished her cry and attended her cheeks with the powder rag. She stood by the window and looked out dully at a gray cat walking a gray fence in a gray backyard. Tomorrow would be Christmas Day, and she had only $1.87 with which to buy Jim a present. She had been saving every penny she could for months with this result. Twenty dollars a week doesn't go far. Only $1.87 to buy a present for Jim.

There was a pier-glass between the windows of the room. Suddenly Della whirled from the window and stood before the glass. Her eyes were shining brilliantly. Rapidly she pulled down her hair and let it fall to its full length.

Now, there were two possessions of the James Dillingham Young's in which they both took a mighty pride. One was Jim's gold watch that had been his father's and his grandfather's. The other was Della's hair. So now Della's beautiful hair fell about her, rippling and shining like a cascade of brown waters. It reached below her knee and made itself almost a garment. And then she did it up again nervously and quickly.

On went her old brown jacket; on went her old brown hat. With a whirl of skirts and with the brilliant sparkle still in her eyes, she fluttered out the door and down the stairs to the street.

Where she stopped the sign read: "Mme. Sofronie. Hair Goods of All Kinds." One flight up Della ran, and collected herself, panting. Madame, large, too white, chilly, hardly looked the "Sofronie."

"Will you buy my hair?" asked Della. "I buy hair," said Madame. "Take yer hat off and let's have a sight at the looks of it." Down rippled the brown cascade.

"Twenty dollars," said Madame, lifting the mass with a practiced hand. "Give it to me quick," said Della.

Oh, and the next two hours tripped by on rosy wings. She was ransacking the stores for Jim's present. She found it at last. It was a platinum fob chain, simple and chaste in design. As soon as she saw it she knew that it must be Jim's. It was like him. Quietness and value—the description applied to both. Twenty-one dollars they took from her for it, and she hurried home with her eighty-seven cents.

When Della reached home her intoxication gave way a little to prudence and reason. She got out her curling irons, lighted the glass, and went to work repairing the ravages made by generosity added to love. Within forty minutes her head was covered with tiny close-lying curls that made her look wonderfully like a truant schoolboy.

"If Jim doesn't kill me before he takes a second look at me, he'll say I look like a Coney Island chorus girl. But what could I do—oh, what could I do with a dollar and eighty-seven cents?"

At 7 o'clock, the coffee was made and the frying pan was on the back of the stove, hot and ready to cook the chops. Jim was never late. Then she heard his step on the stair away down on the first flight, and she turned white just for a moment. She had a habit of saying little silent prayers about the simplest everyday things, and now she whispered: "Please God, make him think that I am still pretty."

The door opened and Jim stepped in and closed it. He looked thin and very serious. Jim stopped inside the door. His eyes were fixed on Della and there was an expression in them that she could not read, and it terrified her. It was not anger, nor surprise, nor disapproval, nor horror, nor any of the sentiments that she had been prepared for. He simply stared at her fixedly with that peculiar expression on his face.

Della wriggled off the table and went for him. "Jim, darling, don't look at me that way. I had my hair cut off and sold it because I couldn't have lived through Christmas without giving you a present. It'll grow out again—you won't mind, will you? I just had to do it. My hair grows awfully fast. Say 'Merry Christmas!' Jim, and let's be happy. You don't know what a nice—what a beautiful, nice gift I've got for you."

"You've cut off your hair?" asked Jim laboriously, as if he had not arrived at that patent fact yet, even after the hardest mental labor.

"Cut it off and sold it. Don't you like me just as well, anyhow? I'm me without my hair, ain't I?"

Jim looked around the room curiously. "You say your hair is all gone?"

"You needn't look for it. It's sold. I tell you—sold and gone, too. It's Christmas Eve, boy. Be good to me, for it went for you. Maybe the hairs of my head were numbered, but nobody could ever count my love for you. Shall I put the chops on, Jim?"

Jim drew a package from his overcoat pocket and threw it upon the table. "Don't make any mistake, Dell, about me, I don't think there's anything in the way of a haircut or a shave or a shampoo that could make me like my girl any less. But if you'll unwrap that package, you may see why you had me going awhile at first."

White fingers and nimble tore at the string and paper. And then an ecstatic scream of joy; and then, alas! a quick feminine change to hysterical tears and wails, necessitating the immediate employment of all the comforting powers of the lord of the flat.

AN OLD-FASHIONED CHRISTMAS

For there lay the combs—the set of combs, side and back—that Della had worshiped for long in a Broadway window. Beautiful combs, pure tortoise shell with jewelled rims—just the shade to wear in her beautiful vanished hair. They were expensive combs, she knew, and her heart had simply craved and yearned over them without the least hope of possession. And now they were hers, but the tresses that should have adorned the coveted adornments were gone.

But she hugged them to her bosom, and at length she was able to look up with dim eyes and smile and say: "My hair grows so fast, Jim!" And then Della leaped up like a little singed cat and cried, "Oh, oh!" Jim had not yet seen his beautiful present. She held it out to him, eagerly upon her open palm. The dull precious metal seemed to flash with a reflection of her bright and ardent spirit.

"Isn't it a dandy, Jim? I hunted all over town to find it. You'll have to look at the time a hundred times a day now. Give me your watch. I want to see how it looks on it."

Instead of obeying, Jim tumbled down on the couch and put his hands under the back of his head and smiled. "Dell, let's put our Christmas presents away and keep 'em awhile. They're too nice to use just at present. I sold the watch to get the money to buy the combs. And now suppose you put the chops on."

The Magi, as you know, were wise men—wonderfully wise men—who brought gifts to the Babe in the manger. Being wise, their gifts were no doubt wise ones, possibly bearing the privilege of exchange in case of duplication. And here I have lamely related to you the chronicle of two foolish children in a flat who most unwisely sacrificed for each other the greatest treasures of their house. But in a last word to the wise of these days, let it be said that of all who give gifts, such as they are wisest. Everywhere they are wisest. They are the Magi.

O. Henry

The Prettiest Packages under the Tree

Homemade Wrapping Paper

These days we tend to think of wrapping paper as something to buy, not something to make; but so many of us make our own Christmas gifts—why not dress them up in our own homemade wrappings? Expensive supplies and complicated directions are not necessary to create beautiful, old-fashioned-looking wrappings.

Something as simple as plain brown wrapping paper can be transformed with a simple bow tied out of plaid florist's ribbon; or for a child's gift, draw puppy prints with magic marker and tie the package with a piece of twine. In place of a bow, try a milk bone.

White tissue paper can also become signature wrapping paper when decorated with glued-on beads in Christmas colors, or a sprinkling of the little silver balls usually used for cake decorating.

Scraps of old floral fabric covered with netting make an elegant wrapping for a special gift; for a more casual presentation, try cutting a sponge in the shape of a gingerbread man and with acrylic paint decorating some simple muslin. Make buttons for the gingerbread men by cutting black felt with a three-hole punch. These packages can be tied with green and red bulky yarn or bright plaid ribbon.

A slightly more complicated wrapping can be made using ferns and colored tissue paper. First, choose a piece of colored tissue paper, then apply a layer of stitch witchery and place the ferns in a random design. Cover with wax paper, iron until secure, and wrap.

Making your own Christmas wrapping paper does take more time than simply buying a box full of generic rolls, but when you see your packages spread out beneath the tree, and you watch the recipients of your gifts pause before they tear through the wrapping, you will understand why wrapping the old-fashioned way is worth the extra effort.

Susan Harrison

Bows Worth Saving
Tying Your Own Bows

Bows are another item easily purchased, but more beautiful if handmade. If you use wired florist's ribbon, bows you always thought too difficult to make become simple and fun to put together.

The flat loop bow, like the one seen on the gingerbread man package on the preceding page, is made by first making one loop, taking the ribbon away from you and bringing it up and back to the end. Hold at the center and make a matching loop opposite the first, again ending at the center. Continue making progressively larger pairs of loops, one on top of the other, until the bow is the size you need. Make one last loop in the center and tie bow with thread or wire.

The pinched loop bow, also seen on the preceding page on the brown wrapping paper, is the most common bow. Begin with five yards of cloth ribbon. Leave twelve inches for the tail and pinch ribbon. (Remember to always hold pinched spots tightly during making of the bow.) Take about eight inches of ribbon and pinch again to form loop. Repeat until approximately twelve inches of ribbon remain. Secure the middle with thin wire and pull loops out to fluff bow. Trim wire, leaving enough to fasten bow to package. Cut a "v" shape out of the ends of the tails or trim ends with pinking shears.

With these two simple bows—and an unlimited variety of ribbon and fabric—your packages will be the prettiest under the tree. And your bows will not be discarded after the holidays, but saved from year to year.

Curiosity

Gay package on the closet shelf
Quite hid away from sight!
I spied it sitting there so still,
All wrapped and ribboned bright!
And then, just once, I picked it up
(No one was there to see!)
It rattled just a wee, wee bit—
This Christmas gift for me!

Was it a toy, or pretty doll?
A painting set, a slate?
How long till Christmastime was here—
Oh, I could hardly wait!
I put it back so carefully
And hid it out of sight,
Gay package on the closet shelf,
All wrapped and ribboned bright.

Georgia B. Adams

A Child's Face

Christmas is a child's face,
Watching from the stair,
Peeking through the banisters
At magic everywhere.

Christmas is a child's face,
Rosy, deep with love;
Trusting, like the wise men,
In the star above.

Christmas is a child's face,
Shining soft and dear;
Believing, with such rapture,
In a cherished time of year.

Christmas comes in many ways
In many homes apart,
But always it's a child's face,
Shining in your heart.

Virginia Covey Boswell

May Christmas day and every day,
for you be very fair . . .
And GOOD LUCK fill the year to
come as snowflakes fill the air.

A joyous Christmas.

Merry Christmas.

For Our Children

Lord Jesus, who didst take little children into Thine arms and laugh and play with them, bless we pray thee, all children at this Christmastide. As with shining eyes and glad hearts they nod their heads so wisely at the stories of the angels, and of a baby cradled in the hay at the end of the way of the wandering star, may their faith and expectation be a rebuke to our own faithlessness.

Help us to make this season all joy for them, a time that shall make Thee, Lord Jesus, more real to them. Watch tenderly over them and keep them safe. Grant that they may grow in love and strength into Christian maturity. May they turn early to Thee, the Friend of children, the Friend of all. We ask in the lovely name of He who was once a child.
Amen.

Peter Marshall

No Sweeter Thing

Life holds no sweeter thing than this—to teach
A little child the tale most loved on earth
And watch the wonder deepen in his eyes
The while you tell him of the Christ Child's birth;

The while you tell of shepherds and a song,
Of gentle, drowsy beasts and fragrant hay
On which that starlit night in Bethlehem
God's tiny Son and his young mother lay.

Life holds no sweeter thing than this—to tell
A little child, while Christmas candles glow,
The story of a Babe whose humble birth
Became the loveliest of truths we know.

Adelaide Love

A Boy at Christmas

If I could have my wish tonight,
It would not be for wealth or fame;
It would not be for some delight
That men who live in luxury claim,
But it would be that I might rise
At three or four a.m. to see,
With eager, happy, boyish eyes,
My presents on the Christmas tree.
Throughout the world there is no joy,
I know now I am growing gray,
So rich as being just a boy,
A little boy on Christmas Day.

I'd like once more to stand and gaze
Enraptured on a Christmas tree,
With eyes that know just how to blaze,
A heart still tuned to ecstacy;
I'd like to feel the old delight,
The surging thrills within me come:
To love a thing with all my might,
To grasp the pleasure of a drum;
To know the meaning of a toy—
A meaning lost to minds blase;
To be just once again,
A little boy on Christmas Day.

I'd like to see a pair of skates
The way they looked to me back then,
Before I'd turned from boyhood's gates
And marched into the world of men;
I'd like to see a jackknife, too,
With those same eager, dancing eyes
That couldn't fault or blemish view;
I'd like to feel the same surprise,
The pleasure, free from all alloy,
That has forever passed away,
When I was just a little boy,
And had my faith in Christmas Day.

Oh, little, laughing, roguish lad,
The king that rules across the seas
Would give his scepter if he had
Such joy as now belongs to thee!
And beards of gray would give their gold,
And all the honors they possess,
Once more within their grasp to hold
Thy present feel for happiness.
Earth sends no greater, surer joy—
As thou, too soon, shall also say—
Than that of him who is a boy,
A little boy on Christmas Day.

Edgar A. Guest

THE
SPIRIT OF CHRISTMAS

This, this is the marvel to mortals revealed,
When the silvery trumpets
Of Christmas have peeled,
That mankind are the children of God.

THE SPIRIT OF CHRISTMAS
137

The Nativity

And Joseph also went up from Galilee out of the city of Nazareth, into Judea, unto the city of David, which is called Bethlehem: (because he was of the house and the lineage of David:) To be taxed with Mary his espoused wife, being great with child.

And so it was, that, while they were there, the days were accomplished that she should be delivered. And she brought forth her firstborn son, and wrapped him in swaddling clothes, and laid him in a manger: because there was no room for them in the inn.

And there were in the same country shepherds abiding in the field, keeping watch over their flock by night. And, lo, the angel of the Lord came upon them, and the glory of the Lord shown round about them: and they were sore afraid. And the angel said unto them, Fear not: for, behold, I bring you good tidings of great joy, which shall be to all people. For unto you is born this day in the city of David a Saviour, which is Christ the Lord.

And this shall be a sign unto you: Ye shall find the babe wrapped in swaddling clothes, lying in a manger.

And suddenly there was with the angel a multitude of the heavenly host praising God, and saying, Glory to God in the highest, and on earth peace, good will toward men.

And it came to pass, as the angels were gone away from them into heaven, the shepherds said to one another. Let us now go even unto Bethlehem, and see this thing which is come to pass, which the Lord hath made known unto us.

And they came with haste, and found Mary, and Joseph, and the babe lying in a manger. And when they had seen it, they made known abroad the saying which was told them concerning this child. And all they that heard it wondered at those things which were told them by the shepherds.

But Mary kept all these things, and pondered them in her heart. And the shepherds returned, glorifying and praising God for all the things that they had heard and seen. . . .

Luke 2: 4 - 20

God Rest Ye, Merry Gentlemen

God rest ye, merry gentlemen; let nothing you dismay,
For Jesus Christ, our Saviour, was born on Christmas Day.
The dawn rose red o'er Bethlehem, the stars shone through the gray,
When Jesus Christ, our Saviour, was born on Christmas Day.

God rest ye, little children; let nothing you afright,
For Jesus Christ, your Saviour, was born this happy night;
Along the hills of Galilee the white flocks sleeping lay,
When Christ, the child of Nazareth, was born on Christmas Day.

God rest ye, all good Christians; upon this blessed morn
The Lord of all good Christians was of a woman born;
Now all your sorrows he doth heal, your sins he takes away;
For Jesus Christ, our Saviour, was born on Christmas Day.

Dinah Maria Mulock Craik

THE SPIRIT OF CHRISTMAS

CHRISTMAS GREETING

May He whose gifts are
blessings true
At Christmastide be near
to you

A Merry Christmas

A Hymn on the Nativity of My Saviour

I sing the birth was born tonight,
The Author both of life and light;
The angels so did sound it,
And like the ravished shepherds said,
Who saw the light and were afraid,
Yet searched and true they found it.

The Son of God, th'Eternal King,
That did us all salvation bring
And freed the soul from danger;
He whom the world could not take,
The Word which heaven and earth did make,
Was now laid in a manger.

Ben Jonson

Twelfth Night

Ever the bells with the news again!
Ever the great star's fire
Is seen above cities' streets
Where every tall church spire
Attests in tapering reach the sum
Of all mankind's desire.

Ever the dreamers . . . to dream again!
Ever the world's heart wakes
To seek across all space and time
The promise Mary makes
In tenderness above her child
As Christmas morning breaks.

Ever the story is told again!
Ever the Magi go
Across the sands to Bethlehem—
Tonight across the snow
The little village churches spread
The great star's afterglow.

Annette Patton Cornell

A Christmas Carol

Everywhere, everywhere, Christmas tonight!
Christmas in lands of the fir tree and pine,
Christmas in lands of the palm tree and vine,
Christmas where snow peaks stand solemn and white,
Christmas where cornfields lie sunny and bright,
Everywhere, everywhere, Christmas tonight!

Christmas where children are hopeful and gay,
Christmas where old men are patient and gray,
Christmas where peace, like a dove in its flight,
Broods o're brave men in the thick of the fight.
Everywhere, everywhere, Christmas tonight!

For the Christ Child who comes is the Master of all,
No palace too great and no cottage too small;
The angels who welcome Him sing from the height,
"In the city of David, a King in His might."
Everywhere, everywhere, Christmas tonight!

Then let every heart keep its Christmas within,
Christ's pity for sorrow, Christ's hatred for sin,
Christ's care for the weakest, Christ's courage for right,
Christ's dread of the darkness, Christ's love of the light.
Everywhere, everywhere, Christmas tonight!

So all the stars of the midnight which compass us round
Shall see a strange glory and hear a strange sound,
And cry, "Look! the earth is aflame with delight,
O sons of the morning, rejoice at the sight."
Everywhere, everywhere, Christmas tonight!

Phillips Brooks

A Christmas Carol

"What means this glory round our feet?"
The Magi mused, "more bright than morn?"
And voices chanted clear and sweet,
"Today the Prince of Peace is born!"

"What means that star," the shepherd said,
"That brightens through the rocky glen?"
And angels, answering overhead,
Sang, "Peace on earth, good-will to men!"

'Tis eighteen hundred year and more
Since those sweet oracles were dumb;
We wait for Him, like them of yore;
Alas, He seems so slow to come!

But it was said, in words of gold
No time or sorrow e'er shall dim,
That little children might be bold
In perfect trust to come to Him.

All round about our feet shall shine
A light like that the Wise Men saw,
If we our loving wills incline
To that sweet Life which is the Law.

So shall we learn to understand
The simple faith of shepherds then,
And clasping kindly, hand in hand,
Sing, "Peace on earth, good-will to men!"

And they who do their souls no wrong,
But keep at eve the faith of morn,
Shall daily hear the angel-song,
"Today the Prince of Peace is born!"

James Russell Lowell

A Nativity Song

How far is it to Bethlehem?
Not very far.
Shall we find the stable room
Lit by a star?

Can we see the little Child,
Is he within?
If we lift the wooden latch
May we go in?

May we stroke the creatures there,
Ox, ass, or sheep?
May we peep like them and see
Jesus asleep?

If we touch His tiny hand
Will He awake?
Will He know we've come so far
Just for His sake?

Great Kings have precious gifts
And we have naught,
Little smiles and little tears
Are all we brought.

For all weary children
Mary must weep,
Here, on His bed of straw,
Sleep children, sleep.

God in His mother's arms,
Babes in the byre,
Sleep, as they sleep who find
Their heart's desire.

Frances Chesterton

The Shepherds Had an Angel

The shepherds had an angel,
The wise men had a star;
But what have I, a little child,
To guide me home from far,
Where glad stars sing together,
And singing angels are?

Lord Jesus is my guardian,
So I can nothing lack;
The lambs lie in His bosom
Along Life's dangerous track;
The willful lambs that go astray
He, bleeding, brings them back.

Those shepherd through the lonely night
Sat watching by their sheep,
Until they saw the heavenly host
Who neither tire nor sleep,
All singing Glory, glory,
In festival they keep.

Christ watches me, His little lamb,
Cares for me day and night,
That I may be His own in heaven;
So angels clad in white
Shall sing their Glory, glory,
For my sake in the height.

Lord, bring me nearer day by day,
Till I my voice unite,
And sing my Glory, glory,
With angels clad in white.
All Glory, glory, given to Thee,
Through all the heavenly height.

Christina Rossetti

The Meaning of Christmas

Wise Men came from the East, perhaps Persia. They saw the Babe—a Babe whose tiny hands were not quite long enough to touch the huge heads of the cattle, and yet hands that were steering the reins that keep the stars, moon, and sun in their orbits. Shepherds came, and they saw baby lips that did not speak, yet lips that might have articulated the secret of every living man that hour. They saw a baby brow under which was a mind and intelligence compared with which the combined intelligences of Europe and America amount to naught.

One silent night, out of the white-chalked hills of Bethlehem, came a gentle cry. The great ones of the earth did not hear it, for they could not understand how an infant could be greater than a man. At the Christ Child's birth, only two groups of people heard that cry: the Shepherds, who knew they did not know anything, and the Wise Men, who knew they did not know everything. Let us reach out at this Christmas season to accept Christ with humility and love.

Fulton J. Sheen

It Is Coming Tonight

The earth has grown old
With its burden of care,
But at Christmas it always is young.
The heart of the jewel
Burns lustrous and fair,
And its soul full of music
Breaks forth on the air
When the song of the angels is sung.

It is coming, old earth,
It is coming tonight;
On the snowflakes which cover thy sod,
The feet of the Christ Child
Fall gently and white,
And the voice of the Christ Child tells out with delight
That mankind are the children of God.

On the sad and the lonely,
The wretched and poor,
That voice of the Christ Child shall fall;
And to every blind wanderer opens the door
Of a hope which he dared
Not to dream before,
With a sunshine of welcome for all.

The feet of the humblest
May walk in the field
Where the feet of the holiest have trod;
This, this is the marvel to mortals revealed,
When the silvery trumpets
Of Christmas have peeled,
That mankind are the children of God.

Phillips Brooks

A Christmas Prayer

O God, our loving Father, help us rightly
To remember the birth of Jesus,
That we may share in the song of the angels,
The gladness of the shepherds,
And the worship of the wise men.

Close the door of hate
And open the door of love
All over the world.

Deliver us from evil by the blessing
That Christ brings,
And teach us to be merry with clear hearts.

May the Christmas morning make us happy
To be thy children
And the Christmas evening bring us to our beds
With grateful thoughts,
Forgiving and forgiven, for Jesus' sake,
Amen.

Robert Louis Stevenson

INDEX

A 1
B 2
C 3
D 4
E 5
F 6
G 7
H 8
I 9
J 0